P9-DNS-580

time for a
BATH

Written and Illustrated by
Steve Jenkins and Robin Page

Houghton Mifflin Books for Children • Houghton Mifflin Harcourt • Boston New York 2011

Do you like taking baths? Enjoyable or not, baths are important because they keep us clean. Many animals also take baths to keep themselves clean. But some animals bathe for other reasons. They may be trying to cool off, warm up, or get rid of parasites. Some take dust baths or wallow in the mud. Others shower in the rain or splash in a puddle. There are creatures that bathe with their tongues or feet. Strangest of all is the ant bath, something you probably don't want to try yourself.

Ahhh . . .

Most **tigers** live where the climate is warm. These big cats cool off by taking a long soak in a lake or river.

The **rhinoceros** doesn't get clean when it takes a bath. But wallowing in mud cools the rhino, and dry mud protects its surprisingly sensitive skin from sunburn and insect bites.

**I'm all dirty —
can I get out now?**

Stand back!

The **emu** also enjoys a mud bath. Afterward, as it shakes off the mud, this big bird gets rid of the parasites that live in its feathers.

Solar power

Spreading its feathers wide, this **vulture** takes a sunbath. The sun's warmth feels good, and the sunlight helps kill bacteria — which is important for a bird that feeds on dead animals.

You missed
a spot.

Some **ants** keep clean
by scrubbing each other
with feet that have been
dipped in the ants' oily
saliva.

Take an
ant bath.

The **pangolin,** an armored
mammal, sits on an ant
nest. It lifts its scales and the
ants crawl beneath them,
eating debris that has
become trapped there.
Then the pangolin lowers
its scales, crushing the ants.
Finally, it takes to the water
and the bodies of the
insects are washed away.

Japanese macaques, or snow monkeys, live in the mountains of Japan. It is cold there during the winter, and the snow monkeys keep warm by soaking in a volcanic hot springs for hours at a time.

How long until spring?

I think I'm going to sneeze.

An **elephant** blows a cloud of fine, dry powder over its body. This dust bath helps keep the elephant's skin free of parasites.

Dusty dancing

The **jerboa** also takes a dust bath. It rids itself of parasites by stamping its oversize feet and stirring up clouds of dust, which cling to its fur.

**It's
not as
easy
as it
looks.**

The **jackrabbit**
likes to keep
its long ears
clean. Using
its back foot,
it bends an
ear down to
its mouth and
washes it with
its tongue.

Don't blink!

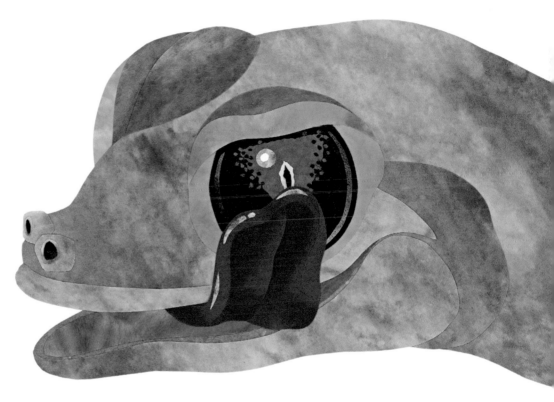

The **gecko** doesn't have eyelids. To keep its eyeballs dirt-free, the lizard licks them with its long, flexible tongue.

Rainy day bath

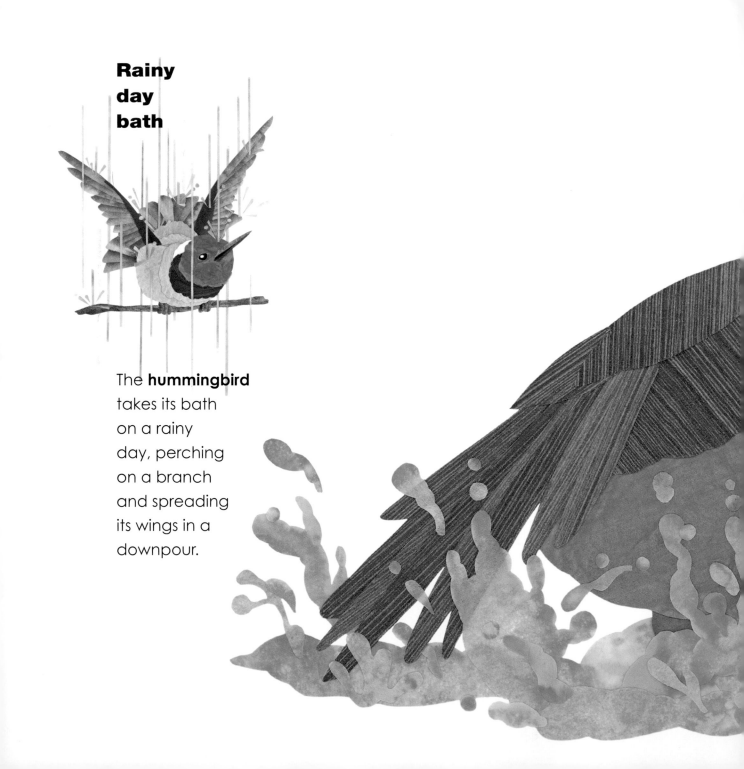

The **hummingbird** takes its bath on a rainy day, perching on a branch and spreading its wings in a downpour.

The **spoonbill** is a messy bather. When it takes a splash bath in a puddle, it flings water all over the place.

Making
a
mess

A **tomato grouper** gets a thorough grooming from a pair of **cleaner shrimp.** To attract the fish, the shrimp do a special dance on the sea floor. The grouper swims in close and holds still as the shrimp pick off loose scales and parasites.

Climb aboard!

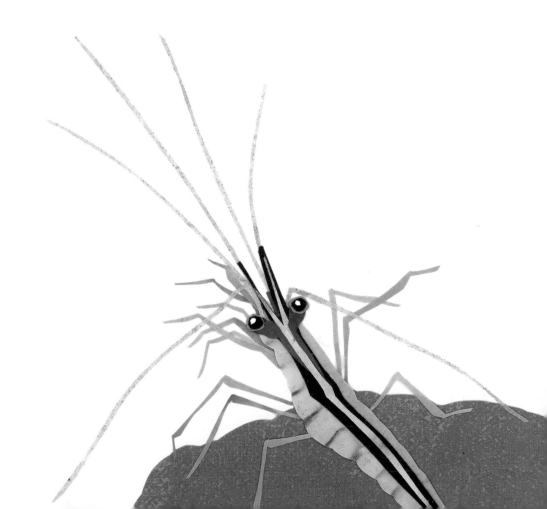

Young **white-tailed deer** bathe by licking each other clean.

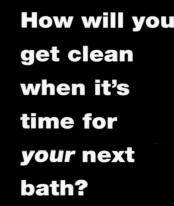

How will you get clean when it's time for *your* next bath?

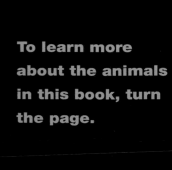

To learn more about the animals in this book, turn the page.

The **Bengal tiger** lives in India and Southeast Asia. Tigers, the largest of the big cats, are stealthy, powerful hunters. A Bengal tiger can weigh as much as 500 pounds (227 kilograms). Only the Siberian tiger is larger. Tigers are meat eaters, and they can kill and eat animals much larger than themselves. Their prey includes deer, buffalo, monkeys, reptiles, and domestic animals. A tiger that is too old or sick to hunt wild game will sometimes kill a human, but this is rare. Bengal tigers are the most common kind of tiger, but there are probably fewer than 2,000 of them left in the wild.

Although it is not as large as the white rhinoceros, its African cousin, the **Indian rhinoceros** still weighs in at an impressive 4,400 pounds (2,000 kilograms). It eats grass, leaves, and fruit. Despite its bulk, a rhinoceros can gallop as fast as a horse for short distances. The Indian rhinoceros is endangered. Probably fewer than 3,000 of these animals remain, living in protected grasslands and forests in northern India and Nepal. Unfortunately, some people in Asia believe that rhino horns have magical or medicinal powers, and many Indian rhinos have been killed for their horn.

The world's second largest bird, after the ostrich, is the **emu.** These flightless birds can stand six feet (almost two meters) tall and weigh over 100 pounds (45 kilograms). Emus live in scrublands, woods, and dense forests in Australia. Their diet consists of grass, seeds, and insects. The bony "helmet" on the emu's head helps the bird push its way through tangled undergrowth. These birds can be dangerous if cornered, kicking out with powerful legs and sharp claws.

The **turkey vulture** has a wingspan of six feet (almost 2 meters). Groups of these large birds circling high in the air are a common sight in many parts of North America. Vultures seek out rising air currents, which they can ride for hours without flapping their wings. They feed on dead animals, or carrion, but will also eat seeds and fruit. As it feeds, the vulture often pokes its head into the bodies of dead animals. A head covered with feathers — like that of most birds — would be hard to clean and could provide a breeding ground for bacteria. Instead, the vulture bakes its bald head in the sun, and whatever has stuck there dries out and falls off.

There are more than 10,000 species of **ants,** found on every continent except Antarctica. For every human on Earth, there are hundreds of thousands of ants. In fact, the combined weight of the world's ants is greater than that of all the humans on the planet. The smallest ants are no bigger than a grain of·sand, while the largest can measure one inch (2½ centimeters) in length. Ants are social insects. They live in colonies with thousands or even millions of individuals. Many ants practice social grooming, washing each other with their mouths or with feet that have been dipped in saliva. As well as keeping themselves clean, this grooming probably helps the ants identify each other as members of the same colony.

The **giant pangolin** is also known as the scaly anteater. It roams the grasslands and forests of central Africa, where it feeds on ants and termites, tearing open their nests with its powerful claws and slurping up the insects with a long, sticky tongue. The pangolin's body is covered in overlapping sharp scales that are made of keratin, the same material as your fingernails. Taking an ant bath, strange as it sounds, helps the pangolin clean the hard-to-reach places beneath its scales. Giant pangolins are about four feet (122 centimeters) long. They protect themselves from leopards and other predators by curling into an armored ball.

 **Japanese macaques** live in the snowy mountains of northern Japan, farther north than any other primate except humans. They are omnivores, with a diet that includes leaves, seeds, fruit, grain, insects, and small animals. They average about three feet (91 centimeters) in height. Japanese macaques—sometimes called snow monkeys—are the only animals other than racoons and humans known to wash their food before eating it. They are intelligent and playful, and have even been observed having snowball fights.

 The **African elephant** is the largest living land animal. A male African elephant can stand 13 feet tall (4 meters) at the shoulder and weigh 14,000 pounds (6,350 kilograms). Female elephants are a little smaller. They live in central and southern Africa and feed on roots, leaves, fruit, and bark, consuming as much as 300 pounds (136 kilograms) of food every day. The elephant uses its remarkable trunk to breathe, drink, communicate, grasp things, and spray itself with dust or water. An elephant's trunk is powerful enough to uproot a tree, but sensitive

enough to pluck delicate fruit without bruising it. It contains more than 100,000 individual muscles. The entire human body, in contrast, includes only about 640 muscles.

 The **jerboa,** a jumping rodent that resembles the kangaroo rat, lives in the desert regions of North Africa, Asia, and southeast Europe. There are several different species of jerboa, with bodies ranging in size from just over an inch (2½ centimeters) to five inches (13 centimeters) long. Some jerboas can cover ten feet (3 meters) in a single leap. The jerboa's tail, which is longer than its body, is used for balance when the jerboa is moving and as a prop when it sits, as it often does, perched on its back legs. Jerboas do not drink — they get all the water they need from the desert plants they eat. Taking a dust bath solves the problem of how to keep clean in an environment where there is little or no water.

 The **jackrabbit** is actually a hare, a close relative of the rabbit. Like most hares, it is large — two feet (61 centimeters) tall — with big back legs and long ears. Jackrabbits live in the grasslands of central and western North America, where they eat grass, grains, and shrubs. Jackrabbits are fast

runners, moving at speeds of up to 40 miles (64 kilometers) an hour. The jackrabbit uses its big ears to listen for approaching predators and as a way to keep cool — as blood circulates through the hare's ears it cools down, helping the hare lose body heat.

 The **web-footed gecko** lives in the Namib Desert of southern Africa. Its webbed toes help it keep its footing on the loose desert sand. During the day, the gecko burrows beneath the blazing sand and rests. It emerges at night and uses its large eyes to search for insects and spiders. These lizards have no eyelids, so they frequently lick their eyeballs to keep them clean and moist. Web-footed geckos are about five inches (12½ centimeters) long.

 Several different species of hummingbird live throughout the Americas. The bird in this book is a **rufous hummingbird.** It is found from Canada to Panama, and is the most common hummingbird in western North America. It is a tiny bird, weighing about 1/10 ounce (3 grams) — just a little more than a Ping-Pong ball. In flight, the hummingbird's wings beat at up to 60 times per second. This is so fast that we can only see them as a blur. Hummingbirds can hover, fly backwards, and even fly upside down. This flying ability helps them

reach the nectar inside flowers, their main source of food. Hummingbirds like to take baths. If it's not raining, they will fly through lawn sprinklers or splash in birdbaths.

The **roseate spoonbill,** a large wading bird, stands about 33 inches (84 centimeters) tall. It is found in swamps, rivers, and wetlands in the southeastern United States and in South America. Spoonbills sweep their flat bills from side to side through the water, straining out small fish, crustaceans, insects, and water plants. The roseate spoonbill's pink color, like that of the flamingo, comes from chemicals in the shells of the shrimp and crabs it eats.

Some fish and shrimp enjoy a mutually beneficial relationship, known as symbiosis. The **scarlet cleaner shrimp** lives on coral reefs and rocky sea bottoms in the warm waters of the Indian and Pacific oceans. It is about two inches (5 centimeters) long. It feeds on parasites and dead skin it picks off the bodies of fish and other animals. The shrimp sets up a "cleaning station" — a prominent spot on the sea floor where it performs a series of special movements. A **tomato grouper,** a fish about 24 inches (61 centimeters) long, notices the shrimp's dance and approaches. The grouper, which normally eats shrimp and small fish, won't eat the cleaner shrimp. In return the shrimp gives the fish a thorough cleaning and gets its own meal.

White-tailed deer are found throughout North and Central America and the northern parts of South America. They weigh between 120 and 300 pounds (54 to 136 kilograms) and feed on leaves, grass, fruit, seeds, and nuts. Male deer have antlers, which they shed and regrow every year. The white-tailed deer gets its name from a patch of white fur on the underside of its tail. Deer travel in groups, or herds. If one deer senses danger, it raises its tail and the flash of white signals the herd to flee.

For Jamie — S.J. & R.P.

Copyright © 2011 by Steve Jenkins and Robin Page

All rights reserved. For information about permission to reproduce selections from this book, write to permissions, Houghton Mifflin Harcourt Publishing Company, 215 Park Avenue South, New York, New York 10003.

Houghton Mifflin Books for Children is an imprint of Houghton Mifflin Harcourt Publishing Company.

www.hmhbooks.com

The text of this book is set in Century Gothic.
The illustrations are torn- and cut-paper collage.

Library of Congress Cataloging-in-Publication Data

Jenkins, Steve, 1952–
  Time for a bath / written and illustrated by Steve Jenkins and Robin Page.
     p. cm.
  ISBN 978-0-547-25037-3
  1. Grooming behavior in animals—Juvenile literature. I. Page, Robin, 1957– II. Title.
  QL760.J46 2011
    591.56'3—dc22
  2010025126

Manufactured in Singapore
TWP 10 9 8 7 6 5 4 3 2 1
4500274340

DISCARD

J 591.56 JENKINS

Jenkins, Steve.
Time for a bath

METRO

R4001354753

METROPOLITAN
Atlanta-Fulton Public Library